Wharton Esherick's Illuminated & Illustrated

SONG OF THE BROAD-AXE

By Walt Whitman

Schiffer Publishing Ltd

4880 Lower Valley Road, Atglen, PA 19310

Library of Congress Control Number: 2010935677

Designed by John P. Cheek
Type set in Benguiat Bk BT/Souvenir Lt BT

ISBN: 978-0-7643-3677-5
Printed in Hong Kong

Published by Schiffer Publishing Ltd.
4880 Lower Valley Road
Atglen, PA 19310
Phone: (610) 593-1777; Fax: (610) 593-2002
E-mail: Info@schifferbooks.com

In Europe, Schiffer books are distributed by
Bushwood Books
6 Marksbury Ave.
Kew Gardens
Surrey TW9 4JF England
Phone: 44 (0) 20 8392 8585; Fax: 44 (0) 20 8392 9876
E-mail: info@bushwoodbooks.co.uk
Website: www.bushwoodbooks.co.uk

Wharton Esherick's
SONG OF THE BROAD-AXE

Wharton Esherick was 33 years old when Mary Marcy, the editor of the *International Socialist Review*, invited him to illustrate her book of children's verse about evolution. It was 1920, the era of the Scope's trial, and this controversial idea appealed to Esherick's politics and sense of fun. He had spent most of the previous decade struggling to make his living as a painter, and it was not working. He had recently begun carving his picture frames and decided to illustrate the book with woodcut prints. Though his carving technique was rough, the prints were both dynamic and whimsical. He enjoyed the work immensely, quickly carving 100 blocks based on Marcy's verses, 78 of which were used in *Rhymes of Early Jungle Folk*, published by Charles H. Kerr Publishing Company in 1922.

Wharton Esherick, c. 1930

Title page of *Rhymes of Early Jungle Folk* by Mary Marcy. 1922.

When *Rhymes* was released, Esherick showed it to Harold Mason, proprietor of the Centaur Bookshop in Philadelphia, hoping that Mason would carry the book. Mason had opened the bookshop at 1224 Chancellor Street in 1921 with the backing of John Frederick Lewis and David Jester, Jr. An intellectual who loved stirring up the sedate world of the Philadelphia society, Mason wanted a salon as much as he wanted a bookstore. The first floor shop stocked all of the latest and best that the literary world had to offer, including whatever was controversial. The second floor was a "private club" where members had lockers for keeping their liquor. During Prohibition the Centaur became the place where the intellectual elite of Philadelphia gathered after hours for cocktails, conversation, and to meet writers. Esherick made the iron and wood centaur that hung outside of the shop for many years. He also carved two woodblocks depicting the Chancellor Street building.

In addition to the shop, Mason hoped to start a press that, according to a Centaur Press announcement, would publish

> ...books that lend themselves naturally to private press production. In carrying out this intention the Press will be governed by two considerations: *first*, the publication of material of sufficient literary or artistic value; *second*, the production of books in a format to merit the attention of the collector.

Philadelphia – Centaur Bookshop, woodblock print, 1924.

Centaur, Wood and iron, 1924. Sign that hung outside the Centaur Bookshop. Now at the Wharton Esherick Museum. *Photo courtesy of James Mario.*

Bookshop, woodblock print, 19**

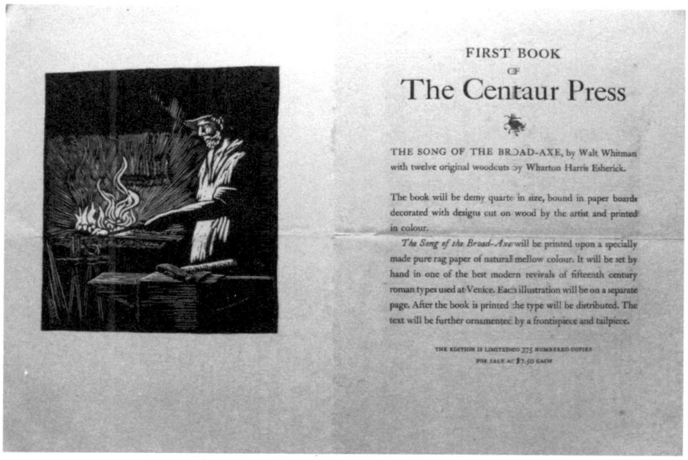

FIRST BOOK
OF
The Centaur Press

THE SONG OF THE BROAD-AXE, by Walt Whitman with twelve original woodcuts by Wharton Harris Esherick.

The book will be demy quarto in size, bound in paper boards decorated with designs cut on wood by the artist and printed in colour.

The Song of the Broad-Axe will be printed upon a specially made pure rag paper of natural mellow colour. It will be set by hand in one of the best modern revivals of fifteenth century roman types used at Venice. Each illustration will be on a separate page. After the book is printed the type will be distributed. The text will be further ornamented by a frontispiece and tailpiece.

THE EDITION IS LIMITED TO 375 NUMBERED COPIES
FOR SALE AT $7.50 EACH

Announcement from Centaur Press about the publication of *Song of the Broad-Axe*, 1924.

Impressed with Esherick's work in *Rhymes,* Mason asked him to illustrate Walt Whitman's poem, *Song of the Broad-Axe,* as the first publication of the Centaur Press. Esherick liked the idea; he had long been a fan of Whitman's poetry. The themes of *Broad-Axe* spoke to Esherick's world view and the path in life that he had chosen:

> The beauty of independence, departure, actions that rely on themselves,
> The American contempt for statutes and ceremonies, the boundless impatience of restraint,
> The loose drift of character, the inkling through random types, the solidification;
> The butcher in the slaughter-house, the hands aboard schooners and sloops, the raftsmen, the pioneer,
> Lumbermen in their winter camp, daybreak in the woods, stripes of snow on limbs of trees, the occasional snapping,
> The glad clear sound of one's own voice, the merry song, the natural life of the woods, the day's work,...
>
> —*Song of the Broad-Axe*

Esherick began carving blocks, approximately 9 x 10 inches, to illustrate the poem. His work for *Broad-Axe* shows his progression from *Rhymes*. He has clearly mastered the form. His woodcuts display not only technical competence, but also an emotional resonance with the tones of Whitman's poem. *The Headsman* exudes a graceful menace and *Whiskey Bar* presents a demoralized desolation reminiscent of a Hopper painting. Esherick complements the symbolism of Whitman's words with allegorical images. He experiments with styles, creating Art Nouveau woodland scenes; *The Hell of War* looks as if it came from a Grecian urn; *A Great City* places a Greek god in the midst of a modern city. He also experiments with light: *The Forger* is illuminated only by the glow of his forge; and *The Hammersmen* are defined by the sparks flying from the pounded hot iron on the anvil.

The Centaur edition was released in 1924. It was limited to 400 numbered copies, of which only 375 were for sale. The book was "printed upon a specially made pure rag paper of natural mellow colour... set by hand in one of the best modern revivals of fifteenth century roman types used at Venice (Centaur Press Announcement)." The boards were covered in paper with woodcut illustrations of trees. The dust jacket featured *Welcome Are All Earth's Lands*, a print that is not included in the book. Esherick also designed and carved a centaur logo for the edition, the first of several that he made for the press over the years.

SONG OF THE BROAD-AXE
By WALT WHITMAN
WITH ILLUSTRATIONS CUT ON WOOD
BY WHARTON H. ESHERICK

PHILADELPHIA
THE CENTAUR PRESS
MCMXXIV

Title page of the Centaur Edition of *Song of the Broad-Axe*, 1924

Carving the blocks for this book seemed to inspire Esherick – he created a hand bound prototype book, with prints made directly from the blocks. Carefully working out an appropriate calligraphy, he hand-lettered the poem. He used illuminated letters to begin paragraphs and filled the spaces at the end of lines with simple line drawings in blue and yellow that reflected the content of the verses. He carved three different tree blocks and placed them where ever there were large blank spaces on the page. He printed a repetitive pattern in green for the cover and bound the corners and spine with brown cloth. The book was a beautiful work of art, 17 x 12 inches, with pages of handmade paper, folded and uncut. He dedicated it to his wife, Letty.

Centaur, woodblock print, 1924. Used as a logo for the Centaur Press.

Welcome Are All Earth's Lands, woodcut, 1924. Used as the dust jacket for the Centaur Edition of *Song of the Broad-Axe*.

Washington Press, c. 1836. Esherick acquired the press from the *Pottstown Mercury* newspaper and used it to print his woodcuts. *Photo courtesy of Mark Sfirri.*

Esherick illustrated three more books for Centaur Press: he carved a porcupine for the frontispiece of *Reflections on the Death of a Porcupine* by D.H. Lawrence (1924); in 1926 he carved a series of delicate vignettes for A.E. Coppard's *Yokohama Garland and Other Poems*; and in 1927 he illustrated the *Song of Solomon*. Esherick's friendship with Mason lasted for the rest of their lives.

Woodcut prints were Esherick's first real success as an artist. They led him to experiment in carving and in working with wood. Through the carving, he realized that he was a sculptor, not a painter. After the early 1930s, he rarely carved woodcuts, pursuing instead the artistic vision for which he is best known – making sculpture that was also furniture. His woodcuts represent an important step in his evolution as an artist and a contribution to American prints. We are happy to be able to make this example of his art available to the public.

The edition you are holding is a reproduction of Esherick's prototype, authorized by the Wharton Esherick Museum. This edition is smaller in size than Esherick's prototype, more like the size of the Centaur Press edition. The original manuscript was carefully scanned and printed using a stochastic method that provides as true an image as is possible. The cover reproduces the print *Welcome Are All Earth's Lands* that graced the dust jacket of the Centaur Edition.

We would like to thank Wharton Esherick's family for their cooperation in making this work available. We would also like to thank Pete Schiffer and the crew of Schiffer Publishing Ltd. for their care in making this reproduction possible.

Paul Eisenhauer, Curator
Wharton Esherick Museum
Paoli, Pennsylvania

Porcupine, woodcut print, 1925. Frontispiece for D.H. Lawrence's *Reflections on the Death of a Porcupine*.

WALT · WHITMAN

SONG OF THE BROAD-AXE

WOODCUTS · BY · WHARTON · H · ESHERICK

·TO · L·N·E·
affectionately
·W·H·E·

"the best-bodied mothers"
·W·W·

WEAPON. shapely, naked, wan!
Head from the mother's bowels drawn!
Wooded flesh and metal bone! limb only one, and lip only one!
Grey-blue leaf by red-heat grown! helve produced from a little seed sown!
Resting the grass amid and upon,
To be lean'd, and to lean on.

Strong shapes, and attributes of strong shapes—masculine trades, sights and sounds;
Long varied train of an emblem, dabs of music;
Fingers of the organist skipping staccato over the keys of the great organ.

Welcome are all earth's lands, each for its kind;
Welcome are lands of pine and oak;
Welcome are lands of the lemon and fig;
Welcome are lands of gold;
Welcome are lands of wheat and maize—welcome those of the grape;
Welcome are lands of sugar and rice;
Welcome the cotton-lands—welcome those of the white potato and sweet potato;
Welcome are mountains, flats, sands, forests, prairies;
Welcome the rich borders of rivers, table-lands, openings;
Welcome the measureless grazing-lands—welcome the teeming soil of orchards, flax, honey, hemp;
Welcome just as much the other more hard-faced lands;
Lands rich as lands of gold, or wheat and fruit lands;
Lands of mines, lands of the manly and rugged ores;
Lands of coal, copper, lead, tin, zinc;
LANDS OF IRON! lands of the make of the axe!

The log at the wood-pile, the axe supported by it;
The sylvan hut, the vine over the doorway, the space clear'd for a garden,
The irregular tapping of rain down on the leaves, after the storm is lull'd,
The wailing and moaning at intervals, the thought of the sea.
The thought of ships struck in the storm, and put on their beam ends, and the cutting away of masts;
The sentiment of the huge timbers of old-fashion'd houses and barns;
The remember'd print or narrative, the voyage at a venture of men, families, goods,
The disembarkation, the founding of a new city,
The voyage of those who sought a New England and found it—the outset anywhere,

The settlements of the Arkansas, Colorado, Ottawa, Willamette,
The slow progress, the scant fare, the axe, rifle, saddle-bags;
The beauty of all adventurous and daring persons,
The beauty of wood-boys and wood-men, with their clear
untrimm'd faces,
The beauty of independence, departure, actions that rely on
themselves,
The American contempt for statutes and ceremonies, the
boundless impatience of restraint,
The loose drift of character, the inkling through random
types, the solidification;
The butcher in the slaughter-house, the hands aboard schooners
and sloops, the raftsman, the pioneer,
Lumbermen in their winter camp, day-break in the woods, stripes
of snow on the limbs of trees, the occasional snapping,
The glad clear sound of one's own voice, the merry song, the
natural life of the woods, the strong day's work,
The blazing fire at night, the sweet taste of supper, the talk,
the bed of hemlock boughs, and the bear-skin;

—The house-builder at work in cities or anywhere,
The preparatory jointing, squaring, sawing, mortising,
The hoist-up of beams, the push of them in their places, laying them
    regular,
Setting the studs by their tenons in the mortises, according as they
    were prepared,
The blows of mallets and hammers, the attitudes of the men, their
    curv'd limbs,
Bending, standing, astride the beams, driving in pins, holding on by
    posts and braces,
The hook'd arm over the plate, the other arm wielding the axe,
The floor-men forcing the planks close, to be nail'd,
Their postures bringing their weapons downward on the bearers,
The echoes resounding through the vacant building;

The huge store-house carried up in the city, well under way,
The six framing-men, two in the middle, and two at each end, carefully bearing on their shoulders a heavy stick for a cross-beam,
The crowded line of masons with trowels in their right hands rapidly laying the long side-wall, two hundred feet from front to rear,
The flexible rise and fall of backs, the continual click of the trowels striking the bricks,
The bricks, one after another, each laid so workmanlike in its place, and set with a knock of the trowel-handle,
The piles of materials, the mortar on the mortar-boards and the steady replenishing by the hod-men;
~Spar-makers in the spar-yard, the swarming row of well-grown apprentices,
The swing of their axes on the square-hew'd log, shaping it toward the shape of a mast,

The brisk short crackle of the steel driven slantingly into the pine,
The butter-color'd chips flying off in great flakes and slivers,
The limber motion of brawny young arms and hips in easy costumes;
The constructor of wharves, bridges, piers, bulk-heads, floats, stays
against the sea;
~The city fireman~ the fire that suddenly bursts forth in the
close pack'd square,
The arriving engines, the hoarse shouts, the nimble stepping and
daring
The strong command through the fire-trumpets, the falling in
line, the rise and fall of the arms forcing the water,
The slender spasmic, blue-white jets ÷ the bringing to bear
of the hooks and ladders, and their execution,
The crash and cut away of connecting wood-work, or through
floors, if the fire smoulders under them,
The crowd with their lit faces, watching ÷ the glare and dense
shadows;

-The forger at his forge-furnace, and the user of the iron after
him,
The maker of the axe large and small, and the welder and
temperer,
The chooser breathing his breath on the cold steel, and trying the
edge with his thumb,
The one who clean-shapes the handle, and sets it firmly in the
socket;
The shadowy processions of the portraits of the past users also,
The primal patient mechanic, the architects and engineers,
The far-off Assyrian edifice, and Mizra edifice,

The Roman lictors preceding the consuls,
The antique European warrior with his axe in combat,
The uplifted arm, the clatter of blows on the helmeted head,
The death-howl, the limpsey tumbling body, the rush of friend
and foe thither,
The siege of revolted lieges determin'd for liberty,
The summons to surrender the battering at castle gates, the
truce and parley;
The sack of an old city in its time,
The bursting in of mercenaries and bigots tumultuously and
disorderly,
Roar, flames, blood, drunkeness, madness,
Goods freely rifled from houses and temples, screams of women
in the gripe of brigands,
Craft and thievery of camp-followers, men running old persons
despairing,
The hell of war, the cruelties of creeds,
The list of all executive deeds and words, just or unjust,
The power of personality, just or unjust.

Muscle and pluck forever!
What invigorates life, invigorates death,
And the dead advance as much as the living advance,
And the future is no more uncertain than the present,
And the roughness of the earth and of man encloses as much as
the delicatesse of the earth and of man,
And nothing endures but personal qualities.

What do you think endures?
Do you think the great city endures?
Or a teeming manufacturing state? or a prepared constitution?
or the best-built steamships?
Or hotels of granite and iron? or any chef-d'œuvres of engineering, forts, armaments?

Away! These are not to be cherish'd for themselves;
They fill their hour, the dancers dance, the musicans play for them;
The show passes, all does well enough of course;
All does very well till one flash of defiance.

The great city is that which has the greatest man or woman;
If it be a few ragged huts, it is still the greatest city in the whole world.

The place where the great city stands is not the place
of stretch'd wharves, docks, manufactures,
deposits of produce,
Nor the place of ceaseless salutes of new comers,
or the anchor lifters of the departing,
Nor the place of the tallest and costliest buildings, or shops
selling goods from the rest of the earth,
Nor the place of the best libraries and schools ~ nor the place
where money is plentiest,
Nor the place of the most numerous population.

Where the city stands with the brawniest breed of orators and
bards;
Where the city stands that is beloved by these, and loves them
in return, and understands them;

Where no monuments exist to heroes, but in the common words and
deeds;
Where thrift is in its place and prudence is in its place;
Where the men and women think lightly of the laws;
Where the slave ceases and the master of slaves ceases;
Where the populace rise at once against the never-ending audacity
of elected persons;
Where fierce men and women pour forth, as the sea to the whistle of
death pours its sweeping and unript waves;
Where outside authority enters always after the precedence of
inside authority;
Where the citizen is always the head and ideal—and President
Mayor, Governor, and what not, are agents for pay;

Where children are taught to be laws to themselves, and to depend
on themselves;
Where equanimity is illustrated in affairs;
Where speculations on the Soul are encouraged;
Where women walk in public processions in the streets, the same
as the men,
Where they enter the public assembly and take places the same
as the men;
Where the city of the faithfulest friends stands;
Where the city of the cleanliness of the sexes stands;
Where the city of the healthiest fathers stands;
Where the city of the best-bodied mothers stands,
There the great city stands.

How beggarly appear arguments before a defiant deed!
How the floridness of the materials of cities shrivels before a man's or woman's look!

All waits, or goes by default, till a strong being appears;
A strong being is the proof of the race, and of the ability of the universe;
When he or she appears, materials are overaw'd,
The dispute on the Soul stops,
The old customs and phrases are confronted, turn'd back or laid away.

What is your money-making now? what can it do now?
What is your respectability now?
What are your theology, tuition, society, traditions, statute-books, now?
Where are your jibes of being now?
Where are your cavils about the Soul now?

A sterile landscape covers the ore ÷ there is as good as the best, for all the forbidding appearance;
There is the mine, there are the miners;
The forge-furnace is there, the melt is accomplish'd; the hammers-men are at hand with their tongs and hammers;
What always served, and always serves, is at hand.

Than this, nothing has better served—it has served all:
Served the fluent-tongued and subtle-sensed Greek, and long ere
the Greek;
Served in building the buildings that last longer than any;
Served the Hebrew, the Persian, the most ancient Hindostanee;
Served the mound-raiser on the Mississippi—served those whose
relics remain in Central America;
Served Albic temples in woods or on plains, with unhewn pillars,
and the druids;
Served the artificial clefts, vast, high, silent, on the snow-cover'd
hills of Scandinavia;
Served those who, time out of mind, made on the granite walls rough
sketches of the sun, moon, stars, ships, ocean-waves;

Served the paths of the irruptions of the Goths ÷ served the pastoral
tribes and nomads;
Served the long, long distant Kelt ÷ served the hardy pirates of
the Baltic;
Served before any of those, the venerable and harmless men of
Ethiopia;
Served the making of helms for the galleys of pleasure, and
the making of those for war;
Served all great works on land, and all great works on the sea;
For the mediæval ages, and before the mediæval ages;
Served not the living only, then as now, but served the dead.

I see the European headsman;
He stands mask'd, cloth'd in red, with huge legs, and
strong naked arms,
And leans on a ponderous axe.

(Whom have you slaughter'd lately, European headsman?
Whose is that blood upon you, so wet and sticky?)

I see the clear sunsets of the martyrs;
I see from the scaffolds the descending ghosts,
Ghosts of dead lords, uncrown'd ladies, impeach'd ministers, rejected kings,
Rivals, traitors, poisoners, disgraced chieftains and the rest.

I see those who in any land have died for the good cause;
The seed is spare, nevertheless the crop shall never run out;
(Mind you, O foreign kings, O priests, the crop shall never run out.)

I see the blood wash'd entirely away from the axe;
Both blade and helve are clean;
They spirt no more the blood of European nobles ÷ they clasp
no more the necks of queens.

I see the headsman withdraw and become useless;
I see the scaffold untrodden and mouldy ÷ I see no longer
any axe upon it;
I see the mighty and friendly emblem of the power of my own
race ÷ the newest, largest race.

America! I do not vaunt my love for you;
(I have what I have.)

The axe leaps!
The solid forest gives fluid utterances;
They tumble forth, they rise and form,
Hut, tent, landing, survey,
Flail, plough, pick, crowbar, spade,
Shingle, rail, prop, wainscot, jamb, lath, panel gable,
Citadel, ceiling, saloon, academy, organ, exhibition-house, library,
Cornice, trellis, pilaster, balcony, window, shutter, turret, porch,
Hoe, rake, pitch-fork, pencil, wagon, staff, saw, jack-plane, mallet,
wedge, rounce,
Chair, tub, hoop, table, wicket, vane, sash, floor;
Work-box, chest, string'd instrument, boat, frame, and what not,
Capitols of States, and capitol of the nation of States,
Long stately rows in avenues, hospitals for orphans or for the
poor or sick,
Manhattan steamboats and clippers, taking the measure of all seas.

The shapes arise!
Shapes of the using of axes anyhow, and the users and all that neighbors them,
Cutters down of wood, and haulers of it to the Penobscot or Kennebec,
Dwellers in cabins among the California mountains, or by the little lakes, or on the Columbia,
Dwellers south on the banks of the Gila or Rio Grande ÷ friendly gatherings, the characters and fun,
Dwellers up north in Minnesota and by the Yellowstone river ÷ dwellers on coasts and off coasts,
Seal-fishers, whalers, arctic seamen breaking passages through the ice.

The shapes arise!
Shapes of factories, arsenals, foundries, markets;
Shapes of the two-threaded tracks of railroads;
Shapes of the sleepers of bridges, vast frameworks, girders, arches;
Shapes of the fleets of barges, towns, lake and canal craft, river craft.

The shapes arise!
Ship-yards and dry-docks along the Eastern and Western Seas, and in many a bay and by-place,
The live-oak kelsons, the pine planks, the spars the hackmatack-roots for knees,

The ships themselves on their ways, the tiers of scaffolds, the
workmen busy outside and inside,
The tools lying around, the great auger and little auger, the adze,
bolt, line, square, gouge, and bead-plane.

The shapes arise!
The shape measur'd, saw'd, jack'd, join'd, stain'd,
The coffin-shape for the head to lie within in his
shroud;
The shape got out in posts, in the bedstead posts, in the posts
of the brides bed;
The shape of the little trough, the shape of the rockers beneath,
the shape of the babe's cradle;
The shape of the floor-planks, the floor-planks for dancers feet;
The shape of the planks of the family home the home of the
friendly parents and children,
The shape of the roof of the home of the happy young man and
woman, the roof over the well-married young man and
woman,
The roof over the supper joyously cook'd by the chaste wife and
joyously eaten by the chaste husband, content after his
days work.

The shapes arise!
The shape of the prisoner's place in the court-room and of him or
her seated in the place;
The shape of the liquor-bar lean'd against by the young rum-
drinker and the old rum-drinker;
The shape of the shamed and angry stairs, trod by sneaking
footsteps;
The shape of the sly settee, and the adulterous unwholesome couple;
The shape of the gambling-board with its devilish winnings and
losings;
The shape of the step-ladder for the convicted and sentenced mur-
derer, the murderer with haggard face and pinion'd arms,
The sheriff at hand with his deputies, the silent and white-lipp'd
crowd, the dangling of the rope

The shapes arise!
Shapes of doors giving many exits and entrances;
The door passing the dissever'd friend, flush'd and in haste;
The door that admits good news and bad news;
The door whence the son left home, confident and puff'd up;
The door he enter'd again from a long and scandalous absence,
diseas'd, broken down, without innocence, without means.

Her shape arises,
She, less guarded than ever, yet more guarded than ever;
The gross and soil'd she moves among do not make her
gross and soil'd;
She knows the thoughts as she passes÷nothing is conceal'd from her;
She is none the less considerate or friendly therefor;
She is the best belov'd÷it is without exception÷she has no
reason to fear. and she does not fear;
Oaths, quarrels, hiccupp'd songs, smutty expressions, are idle to
her as she passes;
She is silent÷she is possess'd of herself÷they do not offend her;
She receives them as the laws of nature receive them÷she is strong,
She too is a law of nature÷there is no law stronger than she is.

The main shapes arise!
Shapes of Democracy. total÷result of centuries;
Shapes, ever projecting other shapes;
Shapes of turbulent manly cities;
Shapes of the friends and home-givers of the whole earth,
Shapes bracing the earth, and braced with the whole earth.

Here endeth the "SONG OF THE BROAD-AXE." written by WALT WHITMAN · First published in 1856 and later revised.

Decorations, lettering, and binding by the hand of WHARTON H·ESHERICK· and wood-blocks printed by him, on a Washington Press at PAOLI· PENNSYLVANIA · September 1924